RECORDED MERCIES:

BEING THE

AUTOBIOGRAPHY OF JANE ANDREW,

LIVING AT ST. IVE, LISKEARD, CORNWALL;

ALSO,

REMINISCENCES OF HER VALUED FRIEND,

THE LATE MRS. DANIEL SMART,

OF CRANBROOK.

COMPILED BY HER YOUNGER DAUGHTER, AS AN AFFECTIONATE
TRIBUTE TO HER MOTHER'S MEMORY.

---

*Any profit arising from the sale of this book will be given to
Mr. Robert and Miss Jane Andrew.*

LONDON:

E. WILMSHURST, BLACKHEATH, AND 10, PATERNOSTER SQUARE.

CRANBROOK: MISS A. SMART, DEARN VILLA.

LONDON:

W. H. AND L. COLLINGRIDGE, CITY PRESS,
ALDERSGATE STREET, E.C.

THE following particulars of JANE ANDREW and my dear MOTHER having recently fallen into my hands, I have felt great pleasure in arranging and sending them forth; trusting they will not only be found interesting, but profitable to those who may read them.

A. S.

CRANBROOK,
  November, 1889.

RECORDED MERCIES.

---◊---

BIRTH AND PARENTAGE.

I WAS born at Lame Barton, in the parish of Egg Buckland, near Plymouth, on June 18th, 1815. My mother was born in Plymouth also, and lived there till her marriage, which was when she was thirty-one years of age. Her father kept a large shoe-making business, made his fortune in a few years, and retired with his wife, one son, and one daughter, who was afterwards my mother. The son (my uncle) got a situation at the Barbican, as land and coast waiter. He was under Government. There he remained fifty years. After that he was pensioned off with a hundred and twenty pounds a year. My grandparents were strict Church people; they attended the old church at Plymouth. The clergyman they heard there was at that church for sixty years—with one book of sermons, containing one sermon for each Sunday in the year. This he used all the sixty years he was there.

DR. HAWKER'S MINISTRY.

Dr. Hawker was preaching at the new church called Charles. He was at that church before my mother was born. I have heard her say he preached the Gospel of Jesus Christ, and did great

B 2

good in Plymouth. He used to be called the "Star of the West." Dr. Hawker was appointed to Charles Church in 1784. This place he filled during his life-time. He died the 6th of April, 1827, and was buried on Good Friday, and on his seventy-fourth birthday. Hundreds were converted by the power of the Spirit under his ministry, and thousands of Christians were fed and led into the truth as it is in Jesus, through him.

But to return to my mother. She used to attend the old church with her parents till she was about eighteen. She was spending the day with friends, who in the evening asked her to go with them to hear Dr. Hawker. She did so, and there the Lord met with her under the preaching, which made her anxious to go and hear Dr. Hawker again. I have heard her say she laboured under the law and a guilty conscience for six months. Then she was set at liberty, under Dr. Hawker's preaching, from these words—"I am thy shield and thy exceeding great reward." She was then enabled to rejoice in the liberty wherewith Christ had made her free.

Now her conflict began. She must leave the dead preaching at the old church and hear Dr. Hawker altogether. She told her parents this, and they were greatly opposed to it. Still she broke through, and went to hear Dr. Hawker for twelve months, and read her Bible very much; from which the Lord, by His Spirit, opened her mind to see adult baptism. She mentioned it to a friend who was a Baptist, and she was soon baptised at Pembroke Street, Devonport (which was the only Baptist place in the two towns at that time). This brought great persecution on her from her parents, who ordered my mother from their presence, and told her she was to go in the kitchen with the servants. She went in and out as a servant for two years, and I have heard her say many times, that she never enjoyed so much of the Lord's presence in her life, as she did during the time when kept under her parents as a slave.

After two years, the Lord gave her favour in their sight, and they both were obliged to own that their daughter's religion must be real in some way, to have borne their reproach and bad treatment as she did.

My father was a farmer's son, near Tavistock, Devonshire. He was converted under a Mr. Rucker's preaching at Tavistock. My father and mother, when they were married, were both well off in the world. They took a very large farm at Egg Buckland, four miles from Plymouth, where three elder brothers and myself were born. Through the Peace (which caused such a fall in the value of provisions), they were obliged to leave this farm. Their leaving made a change in their circumstances, and they had to move about from place to place for several years. My parents had six children, five boys and myself. When we children came to be what is called " sprinkled," it was a great trial to my mother, as she was a Baptist. (My father was an Independent.) Yet they were obliged to submit, as they could not get registers in those days except they were sprinkled at the Church of England, nor could they work under Government. So, as my mother had known Dr. Hawker, was converted under his preaching, and was so near Plymouth at this time, she used to ask him to sprinkle us children, and he did so. He was in the Church of England and had to do his duty, but he never went further in the Church forms than he was obliged to. He used to have the children brought on the Sunday afternoon (often there would be eighteen to twenty children brought at once), and the father and mother alone with the baby—the old doctor would not ask for the sponsors, for there would be plenty of people around. This was the way we used to be christened.

I am sure I was never taken to church in faith by my parents, but only to get a register, as it was required for many things then.

Soon after I was born the times altered, and everthing seemed to be against the farmer, so that my parents soon lost much of what they had of this world's goods, and had great trials, losses, and crosses, all through the remainder of their lives. When I was about six years old, they moved to Buckland Monachorum. We lived there till I was about eighteen, and our parents brought us all up in a moral, sober way.

EARLY CONVICTIONS.

About this time the Lord began to convince me of my state before Him, and for five years I was led on by the Spirit of the Lord working with me in a quiet way. We had no place of truth near; it was nine miles from our farm to Plymouth, where we used to go, when there was an opportunity of doing so, to hear Mr. Triggs, at Trinity Chapel. At that time he was made the means, in the Lord's hands, of much comfort to my soul; and I often used to go to Mount Zion Chapel, Devonport, to hear Mr. Cartwright, who was there at that time. I have heard him with comfort many times. Mr. Triggs, after some years, left Plymouth, and went to Gower Street Chapel, London. The loss of him from Plymouth I felt very much. My parents had to leave the farm at North Buckland, and came to live in a small farm, for growing fruit, at Calstock, in Cornwall. This was about the year 1836. There we had great trials, as the fruit failed that year. My parents, with their family, sought for a place of worship, and met with one at Gunnislake, under Mr. Moseley. There we attended for two years, my soul between hope and despair—up and down—without real peace and confidence in the Lord Jesus as my All.

After this there was a little farm taken, called "Kaison," in St. Ive parish, about nine miles further west, where we all moved in 1838. We had not been there long when my dear father became very afflicted. To move to St. Ive was a great trial to me, as I feared I should not be able to get to Plymouth or Devonport to hear the truth preached. I had a brother at that time who was married, and lived at Plymouth; he was a member of Mr. Triggs' church. Plymouth was sixteen miles from St. Ive, and as there was not a cause of truth nearer I used to travel on foot, when I was able, for the sake of hearing Mr. Triggs. I wished to leave home, and seek my own living, by going to Plymouth to service, and spoke to my parents about it; but I being their only daughter, and they were both getting old and infirm, and in great trials as to this world, they would not agree that I should leave them. Still I tried hard to have my own way and go (not that I wanted to flee from my parents because they were in trial, but my soul longed for the truth, and there was none near to these parts). But the dear Lord, who had marked out my path, over-ruled my mind, and I felt my parents were both the Lord's children; so I remained.

DEATH OF HER PARENTS, AND GREAT AFFLICTION.

My dear father, who had been a great sufferer, died in October, 1840. There were my mother, three brothers, and myself (one brother having gone to America), all left in very straitened circumstances, which caused great trial to the family.

Soon after my father's death I was taken ill, and was laid by from that time for fourteen years. I was visited now and then by one or two Christian friends from Liskeard. I had been seeking hither and thither to find real peace for my soul. But God, who led the Children of Israel forty years through the wilderness, and fed and taught them, had laid me aside by sickness for fourteen years to teach me myself, and to bring me to know my interest in Christ alone, from His own Spirit's power, through the Word.

We moved on together at " Kaison " for three years—my mother and two brothers. There was a temporary living for my youngest brother (Robert) and myself whilst my mother lived. My mother was taken ill and died in October, 1843. Then the little farm, and all that was upon it, came to my third brother, and I and my youngest brother had no more claim there as a home.

My poor, dear mother was only ill eight days, but during the time of her illness I had great anxiety, both of soul and circumstances. I was a cripple, and was seated beside her from the time she was taken, till she died. I felt I had been very rebellious against the Lord in the way He had led us, and the painful circumstances we were brought into.

One day, lying by her side, seeing her in great suffering, that Word with great power and con- demnation was brought into my soul from the eighty- ninth Psalm—" If his children forsake My law, and walk not in My judgments ; if they break My statutes, and keep not My commandments ; then will I visit their transgression with the rod, and their iniquity with stripes." I lay under that for two days, with all the troubles around me, without a Christian friend to speak to, and was too weak and ill to take the Bible to find it. These words brought such terror into my soul that I was afraid to sleep, for fear I should awake in hell. My dear mother, seeing my anguish of mind, asked me what was the matter, and I told her. She replied, " The Lord is about to deliver you from the bondage you have been in for years."

That night the Lord, by His Spirit, came to the room and sounded the remainder of that verse into my heart and ears—" Nevertheless, My lovingkind-ness will I not utterly take from him, nor suffer My faithfulness to fail." By this portion I was brought to feel my union and oneness with and in Christ Jesus. For the time, I had no more doubt of my interest in Christ than if I had been in heaven.

Just as the morning light began to dawn, Satan stepped in, by causing me to look at my mother, and see death in her face. The arrow of my circumstances, with her sufferings and loss, came over me, and the thought that, as soon as her breath was gone, I should be left friendless, penni-less, and homeless, with a dear young brother, who was not then in a fit state to get a livelihood. My dear mother saw this brother in the room. She asked him to go out, which he did, in great trouble. She then looked up at me, with such earnestness and anxiety in her mind. "What will become of Robert ?" I looked at her, and said, "Well, my dear mother, you are not anxious about me—what am I to do ? We shall both be left alike when you are gone." She looked earnestly at me, and said, "The Lord will take care of you. He has promised me He will, though it may be in a way your nature may not like, yet He has promised me that He will take care of you." Looking me in the face again, she said, "I have one thing for you to promise," and then said, "It is that Robert and you will never part while you live." (She had no idea then that we should be kept together forty-eight years, as my life had been despaired of for many months.) I felt she had put a great task on me, in the position we both stood when her breath was gone, and I said, "How can you try to make me promise to remain with Robert, when you know we have nothing to look at but the Union?" She said, "You must promise me." I looked up as simply as a child, and said, "Lord, give me words to satisfy her." And the words came out—"Well, mother, I will do so, as long as the Lord will keep us together." My mother was satisfied, and called my brother to her bedside. She talked to him, and then prayed earnestly for the Lord's protection and guidance over us both, and, above all things, that He would call my brother, by His grace. (And I might here mention that my mother's death was, soon after, the means of Robert's conversion.)

Within half-an-hour of this affecting scene, feeling the burden was all too great for me to stand under, my soul was lighted up with the words the Lord spoke to the Apostle—"My grace is sufficient for thee, for My strength is made perfect in weakness." With this I felt with the Apostle, and said, "Most gladly, therefore, will I rather glory in mine infirmities, that the power of Christ may rest upon me."

By this time (Sunday, mid-day) my mother was past conversing with me, and fell asleep in Jesus about four o'clock in the afternoon. My poor brother Robert was in a frantic state, so that our elder brother was obliged to take him out of the room. Then he returned to me, and took my dear mother from my bosom, where she had breathed her last, and carried me over the stairs, as I was not able to stand any more than a baby. With this I cried out, "Lord Jesus, help me! Thou art my Father and my Friend." With that I had these words—"In all thy ways acknowledge Him, and He shall direct thy paths." And again—"Commit thy way unto the Lord, trust also in Him, and He shall bring it to pass." With this I was brought as quiet as a lamb. I felt all was right. I thanked the Lord He had taken my poor mother to Himself, and felt I could cast myself and my poor brother into His hands. I had that word also—"I will bring the blind by a way that they knew not; I will lead them in paths that they have not known; I will make darkness light before them, and crooked things straight. These things will I do unto them, and not forsake them."

This was forty-eight years ago, and I can now say, and bless the Lord in my soul, that not one thing has failed of all that He then promised me.

PROVIDENTIAL MEETING WITH MRS. REED.

I must now go back a little way. Six months after my father died I was sent to Stonehouse, to a Mrs. Cato's that I might be under Dr. Budd. I would now wish to mention a circumstance, to show the goodness of the Lord in opening a way for my after-years' support. The morning after I got to Stonehouse, Mrs. Cato and I went to see Dr. Budd. While we were away, there was a lady called, named Mrs. Reed (afterwards Mrs. Daniel Smart), who came in through knowing Mr. and Mrs. Cato, as they all attended Mr. Easterbrook's chapel at Devonport. When we returned my appearance struck her—my being in bad health and dressed in black—and caused her to inquire who? and what I was? I, not caring to converse with her, went into another room, when she enquired of my friends all particulars about myself and family. They told her of my mother, and the circumstances of the family. She immediately said to my friends, "Take care of her, and whatever she wants get for her; and I will try and see her to have a little conversation." This she did, and we soon found a home in each other's hearts, in telling of what the Lord had done for us. The doctor said if I remained there under his care, I must go into the hospital. This very much frightened me, so that I soon returned home again.

When Mrs. Reed came the next time, and found I was gone, she was disappointed and surprised. My friends told her my mother would be coming down to see Dr. Budd, to know his mind about me.

Mrs. Reed said, " When Mrs. Andrew comes, you bring her up to see me."

After I had been home a week, my mother had our own doctor to see me; but thought it right to see Dr. Budd, and tell him my objections to going into the hospital. So she went to Plymouth and stayed at Mrs. Cato's, who kindly took her up to see Mrs. Reed. Mrs. Reed was much taken with my mother, and felt for her in all her sorrow. She told her to come there as often as she could, and make her house her home, which my mother did till the time of her death. This lady was a friend indeed, so that neither my mother nor myself wanted till the time of my mother's death. When my mother was ill, my elder brother went to Mrs. Reed, to tell her of it. She wished to have sent a physician, but it seemed like money thrown away ; therefore we did not desire it.

Through my mother being with Mrs. Reed so much during those two and a half years, she knew all the different members of our family and their matters. On my mother's death-bed she requested me to write a note to Mrs. Reed, telling her she was going home to be with Jesus, and thanking her for all her love and kindness since the time she first saw her. Now, I thought to hear no more of Mrs. Reed, as it was so long since she had seen me.

About a month after my mother was buried, my elder brother, who was going to have our farm, wished to get married ; and it was right he should be, as I was not fit to manage his house. He went to have a talk with his intended wife's mother, to appoint the time of his marriage, who said she should not allow her daughter to come there till he had put his brother and sister out of doors. It was quite opposite to my brother's wish to do such a thing as that, so he came to me in great distress, when I was sitting in a chair, helpless as a child. He said, " What do you think ? The old lady will not let her daughter come till I have put you out of doors! What shall I do?" We talked the matter over a bit. I said, "It seems hard; but I will not interfere with her." All at once I heard a voice, as plainly as if anyone had audibly spoken it in the room—"I will fight for you, and you shall hold your peace." This brother was not a Christian, but he understood right from wrong, so I looked up in his face, and said, "My dear, you must not ask me another question about it, for the Lord has just spoken that word to my heart, therefore I have no right to say another word. You must go and manage your matters, and when you are ready to be married take me up and carry me over under the hedge, for the Lord's promise is sure to me—'I will fight for you, and you shall hold your peace.'" But my agony of mind for my poor brother Robert, to know what he would do, or how I could fulfil my promise to my mother, was great. There I was forced to rest, begging the Lord to help me. I had never written to, or heard from, Mrs. Reed since the time of my mother's death.

Two days after this, Mr. Nattle, a Christian minister at our Church at St. Ive (who had been acquainted with all the family matters, and had been a friend to my mother, and visited her to the last), came to me with a letter from Mrs. Reed, which he was desired to bring and read to me, and to write to her again, to tell her all particulars; for she had dreamt about me two nights running, as seeing me in very great trouble, and felt, for my dear mother's sake, she must write and interfere in my case. She desired him to write every particular—the worst—exactly as it was. As I directed him, so he wrote, and vouched for the truth of all that was said. Some days after, I had a letter from Mrs. Reed myself, saying she must see me by some means. As she could see no way of coming to me (as our position at that time was not equal to making one in her station of life comfortable), I wrote to say I would try to come, if I died on the road. She then wrote and told me I was to do so, as she would make every arrangement for my coming ; and also that my brother Robert, my elder brother, and his intended wife, were to come with me, as she wanted to see them all. So I was taken on in a covered cart, on my bed, as far as Saltash ; then Mrs. Reed had made every arrangement with Mrs. Cato to get a cab, and meet us at Saltash, to take me to Mrs. Cato's house, where she was to take care of me till the next day ; that my brothers were to come straight to her, which they did, and she talked to them separately and together. Mrs. Reed had never known what I had promised my mother about my brother Robert, up to this time. She had not seen what Robert could do, otherwise than living with my brother and working for him. She would not make any arrangement with them in any way till she had seen me, as she did not know what my mind was on the subject. She decided, after she had seen me, for myself and Robert to stay there with them for a time—she would pay for my board, and put Mr. Nattle over me to see I was treated kindly. The others returned home again, after she had said she would send for them when she had seen me.

The next morning, by ten o'clock, Mrs. Reed came to Mrs. Cato's, where I was in bed. She looked at me, and said, " That is the face I saw in my dream " (for I was altered since she had seen me two years and a half before). We talked together of things temporal and things spiritual, but as I was so afflicted and weak, she soon said, " This is enough for to-day. I will see you again to-morrow." By this time Mrs. Cato was left a widow, so I remained there six weeks. Mrs. Reed visited me nearly every day, and ministered to me for all my needs.

My elder brother soon got married, whilst I was

at Plymouth. After they were all settled, Mrs. Reed sent for my brothers again, and brought them together where I was. She gave her opinion that, as far as she could see, it was the Lord's mind that I should return to "Kaison" with my brother, and she would take care of me, so that it should cost him nothing, and also pay him for a room ; that Robert was to remain there also, and do what he could for his brother, to earn his provisions and clothes—then I should be able to fulfil my promise to my mother, by staying with Robert, giving him all the advice and showing him all the kindness I could. With this all agreed, and we remained there eight years.

MRS. REED'S MARRIAGE TO MR. DANIEL SMART.

I was still more and more afflicted, not being able to do anything towards getting a living for myself. Mrs. Reed took all the matter into consideration ; she allowed my brother so much a year for the two rooms, and any attendance I required that Robert could not do for me. She continued to supply me with comforts I required from 1843 to 1847. Then Mrs. Reed left Stoke, but still continued her love and kindness. In 1848, she married Mr. Daniel Smart, when she wrote to me very kindly, telling me that she should not be able to do for me as she had done, but she would still do what she could, and be my friend and adviser in what I might require. During the years she took charge of me, I had nothing to trouble me about temporal things, but now I was brought to feel I had the Lord to look to for everything I needed. She wrote to me very kindly, as she knew I should feel her loss, and told me she had been praying much that the Lord would meet me with the letter, and support me under it. I was at first rebellious, and like a wild bull in a net, at losing Mrs. Reed, because she had been my temporal support, and my spiritual friend.   We had had much fellowship and communion together, as she used to have me down with her in the summer for six weeks at a time, and I went there three summers running.   I used to join her then at the chapel, which was the only opportunity I had of hearing a sermon for about fourteen years.

After I had read this letter, and began to consider what I was going to do, this verse was brought to me, just as I had had passages of Scripture before—

> "Blind unbelief is sure to err,
>   And scan His work in vain;
> God is His own Interpreter,
>   And He will make it plain."

I was then enabled to thank the Lord for the friend He had given me in Mrs. Reed, and to pray for her that His blessing might go with her and rest upon her.   I wrote Mrs. Reed a letter, as she requested me, saying how the Lord had met me with her letter, thanking her for all the kindness she had shown me, and feeling we were still tied together with that love in Christ that nothing could separate.   I now felt I had to look to the Lord daily for everything; and I would speak it to the honour and glory of His name, that for more than ten years He sent me support in every way, from many different sources; and I now experienced the blessedness of coming daily to Him as a little child for everything I needed, both temporally and spiritually.

Some months after this, I became more and more afflicted.   My disease turned to dropsy.   I was seven years unable to stand on my feet; the water was drawn from my body by blisters, through the doctor's order.   All this time, Robert and I were going on together with our married brother, he looking to me as his spiritual mother, as he was then seeking the Lord.   He went to Devonport to hear Mr. French, under whose ministry he was set at liberty by these words in Jeremiah xxxi. 9—" They shall come with weeping, and with supplications will I lead them : I will cause them to walk by the rivers of waters in a straight way, wherein they shall not stumble : for I am a Father to Israel, and Ephraim is My firstborn."

Robert worked for our brother. By this time he had a little wages. He also had five sheep, and kept them upon other people's farms, and paid for their keeping. The Lord so prospered his little flock, that in a few years he had thirty. With his earnings he helped me all he could and saved a little besides. He considered that we were both brother and sister by nature, and brother and sister by grace ; so he felt it his duty to do all he could to take care of me, and a strong desire that he might be able to get on, so that we might live together by ourselves.

BAPTISM IN THE SEA.

My affliction increased, and it looked as if I should soon be taken away. About this time, I was brought by the Spirit, through the Word, to see believers' baptism. Many portions of the Word were opened to my soul. At this time I was confined to my bedroom, so that I was not taught it by preaching, yet I saw it was in the Word. But I was then in such a state of affliction that I could not be moved, so I was obliged to ask the Lord to teach me, lead me, and make the way plain for me to go through it. I acknowledged it to be the believer's privilege, and right to do so in obedience to our Father's will. I never saw it as a saving ordinance. However, I was unable to go through it for three years. Then my doctor said one day to me, "I think, Miss Andrew, if it could be possible for you to get to Plymouth, and try the warm salt water bathing, it might be great good to you." I was willing, and I had some friends in Plymouth, so I was taken there, and then went to the baths in Union Street. In less than a month I walked half a mile from where I was staying. When I was able to walk so far, I desired to go to hear the truth preached. The friend I was staying with used to go to a Mr. Snell's chapel, in Union Street. This being the nearest place of worship, I went with her in the morning. After the service was over, Mr. Snell gave out that there was to be a baptising on the Monday, out in the open sea, the other side of Plymouth. Then all the past desires to be baptised went through my mind, and that word dropped into my heart—" See here is water, what doth hinder thee?" I said, "Dear Lord, give me faith and strength as Thou seest I need them, and in Thy name I will go." I made it known, and the next day was baptised with two more as great invalids as myself. I had much joy in it, and great peace in Jesus through His Word, that was made very sweet and profitable to my soul. I found, through it all, that it was the joy of the Lord that was my strength. I have never had to regret it since. Oh, it is Jesus who has been my refuge and strength, and my present help in all my troubles, and He is still all my salvation and all my desire! Oh, bless and praise His dear name, He is my Jehovah-Jireh, the Lord who hath, and doth, and ever will provide for me! Oh, it is of Him, and to Him, and through Him, are all things, to whom be glory, for ever and ever! Amen.

I was temporarily restored by the bathing, but the disease went to my legs, from which I have suffered ever since. We still moved on, my brother looking out with more hope to get a few fields, so that he might work and take care of me. All my other brothers were married, and did nothing for me. Just about this time, when my brother was so anxious about taking care of me (as it was not

pleasant to be with married brothers), we both felt
in our hearts to cry mightily to God about it, as we
saw no way how it could be done. That word was
brought to me—"If thou canst believe, all things
are possible to him that believeth"; and I was
enabled to say with the man in the Gospel, "Lord,
I believe, help thou mine unbelief." Some time
after this, I was still pleading with the Lord that
He would turn our captivity for us, according to
the desire of my brother Robert, when that word
was given me—"Ye shall not go out with haste,
nor go by flight, for the Lord will go before you;
and the God of Israel will be your rereward." I felt
as confident that the Lord could move us from
where we were, as if we had been going out. But
we had to travel on in the same course for seven
years before deliverance came.

EXERCISE OF MIND RESPECTING GOING TO AMERICA.

About six years after this time, we had a brother
who had gone to America some years before, and
had lost his wife, and got into bad health. He was
advised by his doctor to come to England for a
winter. He did so in November, with his two
children. He was in partnership out there, so that
he arranged his matters with his partner for the
security of his children, and brought with him £100.
He came to my married brother's house, where he
stayed the winter. He got better, and seeing the
position of Robert and myself, and knowing by this
time Robert's little flock of sheep was worth £40,
and that I had Christian friends who were kind to
me, he tried to persuade my brother Robert to go
to America with him. Robert said, "I will go, but
I must take my sister with me." He said, "Oh,
no, I should not advise your doing that, as Jane
has good friends here who will not see her want,
and you have money enough to pay your fare out,
and do something with." At this, Robert replied,

"What! do you think I can pick up the little money the Lord has blessed me with, go away to America, and leave my sister upon the hands of other people? No, John, the Lord has made us both one in Christ, and being my sister temporally and my sister spiritually, where I go she must go."

Robert wished to go to America, as he thought he could do better for me there than here. He asked me my thoughts on the subject. I said to him, " Deliverance will come from here, I know, but I do not think it is to go to America ; still, if your mind is made up to go, and you do go, I must go with you, but not believing that it is the Lord's hand that is going to take us there." He was not taught at this time, as he has been since, to look at the Lord's guidance ; but, to be free from where we were, he would at that time have gone anywhere if he could have taken me with him, that we might live together.

All this went on in March, 1854, when my brother John intended returning to America. As I was in such delicate health, the friends all said I should never live to get there. Robert applied to the doctor who had been attending me for years, told him all the case, and asked him if he thought I should stand the voyage. He said, " I could not say, but I would advise you not to take her in the month of March, nor yet in a sailing vessel ; but go in May, and by a steamer, then she might live to get over."

It was all arranged, and my brother began to see about selling off his sheep. My American brother was going to start at the end of March, but, having two brothers in London, he wished to go up and see them before he went. He did so, and took all his money in his pocket in bank notes, as he was going to send his money to America through a bank, except what he required for his passage. When he came to the bank it was too early, and had not opened, so he thought he would go down to the docks to see if there was a vessel going out to Quebec. He saw one advertised to start in three days, and walked round the quay a little while looking at the vessel, when two well-dressed men accosted him, and asked if he was going to Quebec. He said he wanted to. They said they were also going, that they had been in and seen the captain, and paid their deposit money, and as they should be chums together they would go in with him, and speak to the captain. So he went in and agreed for his journey, and for the two children, who were then at his brother's house. He paid his deposit, and wished the captain good morning, who said, " Be in time, for we sail in three days," naming the hour. He and the men came out. They said, " Now we will go in and have a glass upon it," which he foolishly agreed to (not that he was any drinker, for he was a very steady man). One of the men ordered what should be had, and there was no doubt some mixture was put in it, for my brother did not wake for some hours. Then he found the men gone, and that he had been robbed of every sixpence he had, with his watch, chain, pocket-book, papers, and everything. He went to the police, but nothing could be done. There he stood in London, with two children, and not a penny in his pocket. He went back to his brother's house in Bermondsey, where he told his trouble, but he could not afford to help him, or to give him a pound to send him back. So he wrote to us and told us all his trouble, and asked if Robert would lend him a little money to carry him back to his own country.

Before this, my anxiety was very great as to going to America. One day I was begging the Lord earnestly to show me whether it was right for myself and Robert to go—if not, that he would bring about something to upset it, when I had these words given me—" If thine eye be single, thy whole body shall be full of light." The Lord taught me this by the portion, that if my eye was single to the glory of God, and submissive to His will, whether going or staying, that my whole body should be full of light, and that He would show me the way I should take; and from that moment I felt the Lord's mind was that we were not to go. Then this circumstance of my brother's robbery turned up, which caused an upset to Robert thinking any more about going to America, and we felt we had to remain at home. He felt he must lend his brother the money to send him to his home; then he also would be all that short when he arrived there, and perhaps he never might be able to pay it back. Therefore Robert's mind was brought with mine to see that the Lord would have us remain at home, and wait till He had opened a door for us in England. So Robert got twenty pounds and sent to our brother John in London, to take him home, and said we had given it all up, and should think nothing more about going to America. So John returned to his own home at Woodstock, in Upper Canada, and we went on as before. This was in March, 1854.

Robert was not exactly pleased to still remain on where he was, but his thoughts would be still running, "I wish I had gone to America." He would say to me sometimes, "If you had been as willing as I was, we should have gone." But the Lord had shown me it was His hand that had stopped us; and that if it was His will to keep us still where we were, I was content. I earnestly begged Robert might be brought to the same point.

ACCIDENT TO HER BROTHER ROBERT.

We went on till June, when our married brother began to cut his grass. He and Robert were in a field, just above the house, and when it was dinner-time they took up a bundle of grass each to bring in for the horses. One went round by the gate into the court to come out, but Robert came out over the hedge. The weight of the grass threw him over the hedge, the heel of his boot caught in a stone and turned his foot right round. With this he fell to the ground, and saw his toes where his heel ought to be. In his fright he caught up his foot and turned it round, and he heard it go into its place. He fell in the court without being able to move. By this time, my other brother came and saw what he had done, called for help, and they brought him in. I was just come downstairs, for the excitement and trial I had gone through the last few months had made me very ill. I looked upon him where they had him in the passage, and fainted away. When they got me round again, I cried out, "Lord, help me," and with that I had this word—"It is I, be not afraid." I said, "Dear Lord, if it be Thine hand, enable me to kiss the rod and to know the hand that hath appointed it, and may all this affliction be cast by faith into Thine hands, and do Thou cause it to work for our souls' good and for Thy glory." By this time they had sent for the doctor, and got Robert to bed, where he was for three weeks. I attended to him as well as I was able, day and night. But he had not been favoured to see the Lord's hand in all the matter as I had. One day, when I was bathing his leg, he looked at me angrily, and said, "If we had gone to America this would not have happened." I said to him, "Oh, the Lord will show you one day as He has me, and you may have to praise Him that He stopped you from going." About a fortnight after he was able to get downstairs. I said to him one day, "You are looking a little brighter this morning. Have you had a good night's rest, or has the Lord shone in upon your soul with any pleasing remembrance?" He clasped me towards him, and said, "Oh, my dear sister, the Lord has heard your prayers on my behalf, and He has revealed Himself unto my soul this night as being all my salvation and all my desire. I know the way He is leading us is right, and I am now made contented to remain here as long as the Lord is pleased to keep us here." I said, "Well, then, now we shall soon be delivered."

How They were Enabled to Take a Farm.

A few days after this, a person came in who had known my brother wished for a little farm, and said, "Why, Robert, Mr. Wills is going to leave 'Ley.'" He replied, "Oh, 'Ley' is too big for me; I have not half money enough to go into 'Ley.'" So this passed on. Still, we were hearing daily that Mr. Wills was going to leave the farm, and that it was to be let. In the meantime, Robert's leg had swollen a good deal, and we thought it right the doctor should see him, so he thought he might ride into Callington for that purpose. I bound up his leg, and his brother lent him a horse, and he went off. It came into his mind, he said, as he went along, about "Ley," but he did all he could to turn it off, feeling he should like the place but had not enough money to start on it. As he rode up through the town to the doctor's house, he saw Mr. Snell (the steward of Squire Curraden, who was the land-lord of Ley) coming down the street, so he thought to himself in a moment, "Well, I might just ask Mr. Snell if Mr. Wills is really going to leave, and whether the place is promised to anyone." So, as the two horses came together, Robert stopped his, and put his hand to his hat. With this, Mr. Snell said, "Do you want me?" for he did not know him. With this Robert said, "Well, sir, I have been told that 'Ley' is to be let, and I thought when

I saw you coming, I would just ask if it were really so, and whether it was promised to anyone or not?" Mr. Snell said, "It is quite true that it is to be let, but I believe the Squire has promised it." So then Robert said, "Oh, well sir, then there is no harm done." "Certainly not," Mr. Snell said, "but still I should like to know who you are?" He told him who he was, and where he lived, and that he was seeking for a little farm, as he had an invalid sister who could not get her living; that we were both living with a married brother now, but that we would rather have a little place to ourselves. Mr. Snell said, "Who could you refer the Squire to for a character, if this man should not have the place?" "Well, sir," he said, "there are many farmers in the place who would give me a character, and Mr. Hobbers (the clergyman) would give me a character for soberness and honesty; but you must prove my farming, for I have never been to myself, so that anyone could know." Mr. Snell said, "If Mr. Hobbers will give you a character, that is sufficient. Still, I believe the Squire has promised it, but should it not be so, I will let you know." Robert thanked him, and went his way, saw the doctor, and returned home again, when he told who he had seen and what he had said.

The next day we were told that the Squire had let it to the man, so we expected to hear no more about it. This was on Wednesday. On the Sunday, our married brother and his wife went to Quethiock, an adjoining parish to St. Ive, to see a sister of hers, who was renting under Squire Curraden. There they were told that the man who had taken "Ley" had gone over to Squire Curraden the day before and told him he was very sorry for it, but he must give the place into his hands again, for he had not money enough to farm it—so it would now be to let again. When they returned home, Robert and I were sitting down eating our supper. They turned into our room and told us what they had heard. I looked at Robert, and said, " Do you think you had better go over to the Squire to-morrow, and ask him a few questions about it ? " He looked at me, and said, " No, Jane, I shall not move one step without hearing from them. Mr. Snell knows where I live, and it is now in the Lord's hands; the place is too large for my pocket, yet I know all things are possible with God, and if He is pleased we shall have it, He can make the way plain." I clasped my hands together, and smilingly said, " Thank the Lord, He has brought you there, and now may He give us grace and faith to commit all into His hands, and to stand still and see His salvation."

The Tuesday following, my brother Robert was well enough to ride round and see his brother's sheep. I was sitting alone in my room, musing over all that was past, and wondering what was to come, when I heard a knock at the door. When I opened it, a gentleman was there on horseback whom I had never seen. He asked me if Mr. Andrew was at home ? I said, " No, he has ridden out to see his sheep." He said, " Then he is better than he has been ? " " Yes, sir," I said. He said, " I am calling to see him ; can you tell me which way he is gone ? " I asked if I should send for him. He said, " No, I will follow him, if you will tell me which way he is gone." It flashed into my mind in a moment that it was the steward. So I said, " Sir, may I ask if you are Mr. Snell ? " He said, " I am ; and am come to see Mr. Andrew about Ley Farm. Are you the sister that is to go with him, if he goes there ? " (For I was a poor, invalid-looking creature, not fit to look after a farm-house, he supposed.) So I said, " I am the sister to go there, if he ever goes there." So he said, " Do you think you are quite qualified to manage a farm-house ? " I replied, " Sir, I am not equal to the work ; but as to the management, I have always been reared up to it." He said, "I have been to Mr. Hobbers, and inquired all about you both. He has given you such a character, and told me the circumstances altogether, and the motive of your brother's taking the little place, that I am perfectly satisfied, and I have no doubt the Squire will be also. Therefore I hope he will have it, and I hope you will have better health, and be able to go on comfortably together."

I thanked him, and he rode away to see my brother. He agreed what day Robert was to meet the Squire and himself on the place. They met, and it was all settled at once. This was the beginning of September, and he was to take it in the following March. There was a day fixed for both parties to sign the agreement the following week. The land was about forty acres.

We were very anxious, both of us knowing there was but little money. My brother Robert felt it a great undertaking. As he had never been a Christian with great faith, he was not able to cast it all upon the Lord, but kept saying, "I do not know whether it would be right for me to sign it." This drove me daily and hourly to the Lord for His guidance, and I was for days crying, "Lord, increase our faith." That word was brought to me (I felt then it was from the Lord, and I am sure to this moment it was)—"My presence shall go with thee, and I will give thee rest." With this I was confident that it was the Lord's hand that was guiding, and I felt a strong faith, and was enabled by the power of the Spirit, to throw all the matter into the Lord's hand ; feeling that He had opened the door, and He who carried us in would carry us through. Not that I thought we should be without trouble, but that all things were possible with Him, and that to Him we should be able to look. From this time till the time we came into the place, was a very anxious one for both of us, and our cry was to the Lord, that He must help us, or we should not be able to stand. For our desire was to meet everything as it came, and not to bring anyone into any trouble through our coming here, or to bring any dishonour upon God or His cause. I had many precious promises through the winter, and, feeling I had the Lord Jesus with me in all things, I was enabled sometimes to smile at the storms that might come upon us.

Elijah's Raven, or Jonah's Ship?

Many of our Christian friends felt it was a great undertaking for my brother, as he was not very strong in body or mind. A very dear friend and cousin wrote me a letter, when he heard of it (knowing my health was so bad I could do no work), and asked me the question, "Whether it was Elijah's Raven, or Jonah's ship?" This I pondered in my mind which it could be. Jonah, I felt, had run from the presence of the Lord, so he was brought into a storm; but Elijah went to the brook by the command of the Lord, and there he was fed by the raven. So I wrote back and said, "I was certain it was not Jonah's ship, as we were made to feel the Lord was with us in everything that had been done; therefore I looked upon it that we were like Elijah, that the Lord was going before us, and that he had caused this place to be let to feed us both, as much as he prepared the ravens to feed Elijah." Then I named this portion to my cousin, which had been given me seven years before—"Ye shall not go out with haste, nor go by flight: for the Lord will go before you; and the God of Israel will be your rereward." Now I was brought to feel after waiting seven years, that this was the Lord opening the way, and that He would be our rereward, by following us after. With this my cousin said no more; but he is still living, and could prove that it has been Elijah's raven, and not Jonah's ship. And we are able, whenever we meet, to rejoice together, giving all the glory to Father, Son, and Holy Ghost.

FAVOUR IN THE SIGHT OF MAN.

We felt great anxiety about the £20 lent to our brother John. Robert began to value up his sheep, feeling he must sell part of them to buy other things. He saw the Lord's hand in his selling them—they made pounds more than they were valued at. With the tenant who was leaving, it was as if the Lord had given us favour in the old man's sight ; for the day the old gentleman had his sale, he said to the auctioneer, " Do not be too particular with Mr. Andrew, respecting what he may want to buy here, for he is a quiet fellow. He and I have gone on very well all the winter, and I wish to go out and give him any privilege I can, and I hope he will do well."

When Mr. Wills had his sale for his furniture, I was brought down to see whether there was anything that would do for us, for we had everything to buy. It was the same auctioneer. The old farmer said the same to him about me and the furniture as he did about my brother and the cattle, for I bought many things through the house for pounds less than they had been valued at. So in all this we saw the Lord's hand going before.

" IT IS THE LORD'S DOING."

We came in on March 23rd. By the time we had looked about a bit, Robert began to find his money was getting short, and many things more were wanted, so we had daily to cry to the Lord for His help. As we moved on, we found that the Lord sent us things in a wonderful way, so that we were able to say, "It is the Lord's doing, and it is marvellous in our eyes."

In the month of May we wanted two cows. I had written out to my brother in America, to tell him that Robert had taken a farm, and that he would want his money as soon as he could conveniently send it. Still, we doubted whether it would come. But the Lord was beforehand. There was a fair at Liskeard in the middle of May. Robert had it on his mind to go there, but feared the money would not come from America. But the week before, we had a letter from my brother John, with an order for the twenty pounds and two pounds interest added to it. This made us both weep before the Lord, because we had doubted whether he would send it ; but in this we saw the Lord's hand also. So Robert was able to go to the fair, and buy the two cows, and had his interest left then ; for cows and calves were cheaper then than they have been since.

We moved on, and had our small harvest with a happy feeling that we were brought to ourselves in a little quiet home. My brother worked hard, as he could not afford to employ a man. A nice old woman was put in my way, as a servant, who was more like a mother to me, and lived with us nine years. Her love for us was so great that she would save and do all she could, as if we were her children. This I felt a gift from the Lord, as I have always been in a delicate state of health.

Friends came and continued their kindness, and put little things about the house, such as we could not afford to buy. One friend at Plymouth spoke to me about taking in lodgers ; but I said to her, " My furniture and house are not fit for lodgers." She said, " I, and my husband and son, will come first." This she did, and stayed a month, and when she returned she made it known to a few of my Christian friends that she had been here. From this, there were many Christian friends who came—some a fortnight, some a month, and some longer. They all bore with the plainness of my furniture and house. We had their Christian fellowship, and they paid us well for being here, which was a great help in getting more comforts around me. This I have continued up to the present time, more or less, as my age and the frailties of my body will admit.

Many have died away, and a few fresh ones come up in their place. All this has been a comfort both spiritually and temporally to ourselves, as well as to them. Some of our old friends were rejoiced, and were able to see the Lord's hands with us; and hundreds of times, when joining with one friend or another, they have been able to praise the Lord for His great mercies and loving kindness year after year.

We had a very tidy harvest the first year, for which we were very thankful.

Many, very many, wonders has the Lord worked for us, which would swell this narrative too much to name, as my wish altogether has been, if ever such a thing as this were published, that it might be for the glory of God, and for the comfort of any of the Lord's children who may read it.

WHAT FRIENDS THOUGHT OF THE UNDERTAKING.

Some of our dear friends were rather indignant at my brother taking a place so large, with the little capital they knew he had; for we never either of us kept anything from our true friends. They said Robert should have remained as he was, and not have entered into business. Some said it was the pride of his heart—that he did not like to see his sister maintained by other people. But they were wrong—it was not pride, but principle; for he felt that as the Lord had saved his soul, and through

me he had been greatly blessed in spiritual
knowledge, it was his duty, as well as his
privilege, to do what he could, in the name of the
Lord, for one of the Lord's children. This principle the Lord alone has bestowed upon us both.
Many of our friends have been brought to acknowledge the wonderful love of the Lord's dealings
with us, both in providence and in grace.

One friend, who could not see that Robert had
done right, came here to see me after we came in.
I was speaking to her of seeing the Lord's hand
and His dealings in bringing us here. With this,
she looked earnestly at me, and said, "Well, Jane,
do you think you have got out of trouble by
coming here?" I said, "No, I cannot think that.
I must get out of the world before I think that, for
God has said in His Word, 'In the world ye shall
have tribulation.' So I expect that, go where I
will." "Well, then," she said, "what shall you say
if you get more trouble and affliction here than you
have had?" "Say?" I replied; "I know I shall
prove that the Lord's love and faithfulness is able
to carry us through whatever trouble He may see
good for us. Therefore it will never lessen the
trouble we may have, our seeing that it is the
Lord's hand that has brought us here." She said
no more; but is still living, and knows and has
acknowledged that it must be the Lord, or we
should have sunk under it.

Another Christian sister said one day, when
talking about my brother labouring so hard (as he
had been obliged to do), "Well, I have never been
able to see the Lord's hand so much as you have
talked about." I said, "Perhaps not, but we have
told you all our matters, and how we were brought
here, and I should have thought you would have
been convinced that it was the Lord's way." I
told her I saw the Lord's hand as much in it as
ever Gideon did when the fleece was turned twice.

She replied, very haughtily, "Well, I must have seen the fleece turned, and turned, and turned again, before I could have entered into such an undertaking as Robert has." "Why, bless you," I said, "I saw the fleece turned, and turned, and turned again, and tasted some of the broth that was poured on the rock, which has strengthened me, and helped me on to the present moment, and I believe that promise will still be fulfilled to our journey's end—'The Eternal God is thy refuge, and underneath are the everlasting arms.'" She said no more; but she is still living, and has many times acknowledged to some of my other friends what wonders the Lord has done for us.

A GREAT TRIAL AND A WONDERFUL DELIVERANCE.

In November we needed a new cow, and my brother went to Launceston on the 14th of the month to buy a cow and calf. It was hard work to gather up money enough for him to take, but he walked away twelve miles, during which time my eyes, I trust, were up unto the hills from whence had come all our help. I begged the Lord to go with him, and put that in his way that he needed. He returned before I expected him, with a cow and a calf. When he came in he was very fatigued, and sat down and wept. I inquired what was the matter. He said, "I have had nothing to eat since I left, except the sandwich you put in my pocket, for it took every farthing I had to buy the cow and calf." I soon refreshed him with a cup of tea, and we were able to thank the Lord together for His preserving care in bringing him safe home.

The cow was all right till Christmas, when we saw there was something the matter with it. We gave it some drenches, but in a few days it died. This was a great trial, which my brother felt very much, as we could see no way in which we could get another. But my faith was strong in the Lord, who had promised that " His presence should go before us, and He would give us rest." I talked to my brother as he sat in the chair, feeling in himself he could go no further, and as I felt so I spoke to him. I said, " The Lord has not brought us thus far to put us to shame. The Lord knows that we have need of another cow, and as sure as you and I are here, in due time He will send us another by some means." I took up the Psalm Book, and I said, " We will read a Psalm together." I read the eighteenth, and when I came to that verse— " Who is worthy to be praised?" I was obliged to stop ; and I looked at my brother, and said, " We have to praise the Lord for this trial, for I am sure there is blessing to come out of it."

My dear old friend Mrs. Reed, who I have spoken of before, was married to Mr. Daniel Smart, and had a family, but we had always communicated together, letters passing every other week. Her circumstances, through marriage, had altered, so that she had not been able to do for me what she had done. Still, her love and thoughts for and about us were the same as ever. I had not the heart to tell her our trouble, feeling it would only be a trial to her mind. But the following morning I had a letter from her, with an order for half-a-sovereign, and saying in her letter that her mind had been greatly exercised that we had been in trouble. (The morning she had written that letter our cow died.) She told me in the letter, that morning she had been pleading with the Lord to open up some way for her own circumstances, and in a moment her mind was turned upon us, and she felt she must pray for us, feeling we must be in trouble. She had now written to desire me to tell her what was the matter, and how we were moving on. I did not write to tell her that day, feeling it would grieve her, yet I felt I must write to thank her for what she had sent. So I wrote her a note, but said nothing about what had happened. I sent it to the post, but the post had gone; therefore I could not send it off till the following day. Our letters crossed each other, and the next morning I received one from her, with an order for two pounds ten shillings, saying that since the time she wrote to me last, she had received from her father (who was a wealthy man in Kent) a present of forty pounds. She knew we were in trouble, so she sent the enclosed to us. Then I had to write her a letter, telling her all the circumstances. I always used to write and tell her all that was going on, as she had known all the circumstances of our coming into this place, and had always a desire with us with one heart before the Lord.

From that opening, from one friend and another, as it was known, so they sent in their presents. We had two or three very dear friends in Liskeard. The day the cow died my brother went to Liskeard, and in the street he met two of my lady friends, who spoke to him, and asked how I was. He said, " Not very bright in body, but, I believe, as happy in the Lord as can be." So the elder sister said, "Why, Robert, you are looking haggard. What is the matter ? " He told them all the trouble. They asked him, before he left the town, to call, as they had something for me. When he called, they talked to him of the Lord's mercies, and how they had known some trials in their day. They cheered him, and gave him a five-pound note as a present from both; and that he should not feel diffident in taking it, they told him that there was a time when they should have been glad of such a thing themselves. In the evening another of my acquaintance called to see these same ladies, and sat talking with them. She asked them if they had heard from me, and how I was. They were able to say they had seen Robert, and they told her all that had happened. She smiled, and said, "Oh, then, now I know why the Post Office was shut before I could get there." And she told them she had written a letter, intending to send five pounds to Mr. Müller, when she arrived at the Post Office and found it shut. "Now," she said, "I shall ride to "Ley" to-morrow, see Jane, and leave it there." Twenty-five pounds was made up in all from various friends, which bought another cow, and we had many pounds left. I felt, in receiving all these things, that word which the Lord gave me at my mother's death—"Commit thy way unto the Lord ; trust also in Him, and He shall bring it to pass."

A Sweet Harvest Thanksgiving.

We moved on through 1856, things appearing to prosper in a wonderful way. That year we had a very good harvest. We were talking over, and feeling how gracious the Lord had been to us, and what wonders He had done for us that year, and we praised Him with all our heart. That word was brought to me—"Come, all ye that fear God, and I will declare what He hath done for my soul " —and we could add, "our bodies too." After the harvest was all over, and the stacks thatched, I said to my brother one evening, after reading the Word together, "What do you think about having a harvest meeting here in our kitchen?" He said, "But how should we carry it out?" I said, "Invite a few Christians all round here—say ten or twenty, if we can find them—and have an afternoon meeting for prayer, reading the Word, and singing. Then have an hour and a half for a cup of tea, and a walk round, to see what God has done for us. Then have a meeting in the evening, and let the brethren speak as they feel led. Tell them what our minds are when they are invited, and that it is simply our desire to glorify the Lord in all that He has done for us." I wrote round to Liskeard, from which we had five, Plushabridge six, Callington ten, Amp and Stoke Linton eight, Gunnislake five. We invited several from the larger towns of our own friends—as many as we could find beds for. We fixed it for the 14th of October. Our cousin, Mr. Rowe, at Millbrook, and his wife, came to guide the meetings, and to speak a little of our being brought into the place, as he had known all about it. All that were invited came. We had such meetings, with the presence of the Lord—it was felt from heart to heart that Jesus was in our midst. It was guided in a wonderful way, through the power of the Spirit. Some brethren prayed, some read, some gave out hymns, and some spoke. All were edified, and able to rejoice. My brother closed the evening meeting with prayer, the first time he had ever been heard by a stranger. Some are living that would testify to the reality of this meeting. Several old Christians said that they had never felt the power of the Spirit so much in a meeting before; but many of these are fallen asleep. We continued these meetings after every harvest for more than twenty years, till, through age and affliction of body, I was not able to attend to it, and many we so much loved in the Lord Jesus had died, and others moved away to different parts, so that we felt we must give them up. But it was with great reluctance, as we had felt so much of the Lord's presence here, and so much blessing to ourselves. Still, the Lord knew our motives, and we were obliged to give them up.

A HOT SUMMER AND ITS EXERCISE OF FAITH.

The year 1858 was a very hot, dry summer. Corn was very scarce—hardly any straw to be seen. There were scarcely any turnips or mangolds. When the corn was brought to the stack-yard, it looked about one-third less than what we had before. It put my brother in great trial of mind how he was going to pay his way, before any other return could come in from the farm ; for there were no turnips to feed a bullock or a sheep. I felt that all this was a great trial for him. I did and said all I could to comfort him. I could not give him faith ; but I cried to the Lord to give us both faith still to cast ourselves upon Him. I was one day going to write a letter to a friend, and just before beginning I was sitting opposite where the stacks were. I looked up, and thought it no wonder that my poor brother was in trouble, and it came in upon me like a flood ; and I cried out to the Lord to take it away from me, and enable us to cast ourselves upon Him. I could plead with the Lord that He had brought us here, and I must still look to Him to help us through, when the word dropped into my heart as if anyone had spoken it into my ears—"And he said unto her, There is not a vessel more. And the oil stayed." I said, "Lord, if this be from Thee, let me hear the word again." I had the words the second time—"And he said unto her, There is not a vessel more. And the oil stayed." I turned to my Bible, which was close at hand, and found the portion, and felt a pleading with the Lord that He could make that bit of corn hold out till there was not a debt left ; and I felt such faith in God about it, that it would all be right according to His Word—"In Me is thy help found." I went to my brother in the field at once, and tried to cheer him, the same as I had been cheered ; but this I could not do, as "Power belongeth unto God." He looked at me, and said, "Well, my sister, be it unto us according to thy faith. But I cannot see how we are going through the year." In the evening we read the chapter, and prayed to the Lord to give us faith and confidence in Himself. So we moved on, the Lord cheering us by His Word, and giving us help from one source and another. The corn and cattle we had to sell were making more money. After the poor harvest, my brother said, "We shall not have any harvest meeting now." I said, "What! No harvest meeting! We have got food for the cattle, and bread for our daily use—and not thank the Lord for it?" So we called the same number together, and they all came. One preached in the evening from that word—" Have faith in God." A blessed time we had. We could praise the Lord for what He had given us, and felt we could trust Him for what was to come.

When harvest was over, I made up the little annual accounts, and found that the bad harvest had paid the year's accounts. Though there were no turnips to feed the bullocks, yet that year's expenses had been met.

We moved on till January, 1859, when I was taken seriously ill, and was under the doctor for two months. This was a great trial to our fleshly minds, and unbelief would often say, " How is it all going to be met?" When I got better, I was ordered to Plymouth, for sea-bathing, which was a further expense. Yet, amidst all, I was often able to plead with the Lord, and to feel that He could help us. Soon harvest came on, and that year was a much more prosperous one.

FEEDING ON THE WORD.

We went on in one way for four or five years, seeing the Lord's hand as we moved on. I was better in body, and we went to the different meetings together now and then, there being no place of truth nearer than four miles. Just at that time we attended at Callington.

Soon after, a very excellent man was at Liskeard, who had left the Church of England.

His name was Mr. Morshead; he preached at the Baptist Chapel. We went there and heard him now and then, when we could, and found food for our souls; this continuing for about eight years, and it proved a very profitable time, spiritually, for us both, as his was a ministry we hear little of in the present day. He was then taken home to be with Jesus. From that time to the present I have been but very little anywhere; but my brother has got about, where he thought he could pick up a crumb now and then. I have felt the Lord has been very gracious, in teaching me from His own Word, when I have been quiet at home alone.

DEATH OF MRS. DANIEL SMART.

In October, 1867, I had a very great trial, in hearing of the death of my dearly beloved friend, and almost mother, Mrs. Smart, of Cranbrook. This I felt exceedingly for some time. I had never known any of her family, only as she would name her husband and children in writing to me. I felt now that all the happiness of even receiving letters from her was gone. I felt I knew nothing of the family, therefore I should hear no more of them, or of her remembrance. But in this I was mistaken, as the Lord's hand was going before me still. I soon received a letter from her eldest daughter. I had had the "Gospel Standard" from Mrs. Reed, from the time she married Mr. Smart to her death. I soon found the "Standard" came as usual, every month. In her love, Mrs. Smart used to send me ten shillings on my birthday (as I was born the 18th of June, the same day her first husband rode into the field of Waterloo, in Blücher's party), which still continued to come. Miss Smart still continued to write to me about the family, and how they were, and would send me her father's sermons when they came out. I also found I was remembered at Christmas by them. This has continued up to the present time. Miss Smart thought she should like to see her mother's dear friend, that she had heard so much about; so after her father's death in April, 1888, she was at liberty to do so, and came to see me the following June. It now being forty years since the time I had seen her mother, the joy of seeing one of my dear friend's offspring was very great to me, and we spent a happy fortnight together.

CONCLUDING REMARKS.

It was the request of Mrs. Smart, twenty-six years ago, that I should write some account of my life, at which time I had no desire that my name should appear in public, as I feared there might be many things in it that would be hardly credible to some minds that might read it. I had never seen it clearly to be the Lord's will that I should do it. When the request was made again by one of my dear friend's children, I thought it over, and felt it rather singular that the request should be made again. I then consented, after much prayer and anxiety before the Lord; and I begged, if spared to do it, that it might be alone to the glory of the Lord, who had done so much for me; and I believe I can truthfully say that every word of the foregoing has been the Lord's dealings with us. Much more, very much more, might have been said of His dealings with our souls. This we can say, that He has been our Teacher, our Leader, and our Guide; and that not one thing has failed of all that He hath promised us. But we feel it is very much more than we deserve.

In 1869 I had a very heavy illness, which was a very great expense, and a sore trial to my brother. Yet we were brought through, and it was one of the best illnesses I ever had for my soul's comfort and profit.

From this we moved on year after year, sometimes with prosperity, and sometimes with adversity—feeling the Lord's blessing from year to year —desiring to walk humbly and with child-like simplicity before Him who was all our salvation and all our desire.

We are now in the year 1889. Many friends have died, and there are many living who have been witnesses to all that I have said. I am now come to the age of seventy-four, and my brother is sixty-nine. We are now looking forward to the time when we shall hear the voice of Jesus, saying, " Come up higher." And we fall down before Him with poor old Jacob's words—" Few and evil have the days of the years of my life been."

I can speak to the praise of my gracious God and Father in a precious Christ Jesus, who hath led me all through my path in this wilderness to the present moment, and I often cry out now with the poet—

> " Oh ! for a heart to praise my God,
>   A heart from sin set free."

The Lord has led me, fed me, and clothed me. Not one good thing has failed of all the Lord my God hath promised me. As to all my trials and afflictions, which have been neither few nor small, they have all been sent for my soul's good, and for the glory of my three-one God in covenant—Father, Son, and Holy Ghost. Oh ! I can now say from my heart, before a heart-searching God, that I would not have been without all I have passed through, both temporally and spiritually, for they have been sanctified by the Eternal Three to my soul's good, and it has been made plain in my experience—the truth of the Word and promises of the Bible. I have known often, in the deepest trials and great sufferings of body, to have faith given me to rest in God and feel all was well ; and in times of need the Lord has applied His Word and promises with such power, that I have often been brought down at His dear feet like a child—made willing to be anything or nothing, that Jesus might be All in All unto my soul. Oh! I can now often look back over the way the Lord hath led me, and feel now, while writing this, how I should like to be able to count up the precious promises I have had brought to my heart and soul in trials and afflictions ; and often when Satan has come in like a flood, the Lord Jesus has lifted up Himself, by His Spirit through some precious word and promise, which has made me rejoice, and say to mine enemy " Rejoice not against me, for though I fall, I shall arise, and though I sit in darkness, the Lord shall be a light unto me." Oh, bless His dear name, He is my light and my salvation ! The Psalms have been made very sweet and precious to my soul very, very often ; also the Prophet Isaiah has been blessed greatly to my soul. Oh, I can say I have had my portions out of the whole Word of God !

Our earnest desire is that " the blessing of the Lord, that maketh rich, and addeth no sorrow with it," may rest upon this little account, and that the Spirit of the Living God may take of the things of Jesus and reveal them unto many souls, or any soul, who may read it. Oh, may it be for the glory of God, in whom is all my help found, for all my springs are in Him ! I would desire to glory in all my infirmities in the writing, so that the power of Christ may rest on my soul in it, and on it, to any who may read it.

Now I am old and grey-headed, and feel that I am near my journey's end and to my Father's house above. My desire and cry to the Lord is, that as the outward man decays, so the inward man may be renewed day by day. Unto Father, Son, and Spirit be all the praise and glory. Amen.

REMINISCENCES

OF

THE LATE MRS. DANIEL SMART.

———◆———

I WOULD desire to add to my little account of my life up to this time, a short account of the lady I have had to mention so often in it—namely, Mrs. Reed—and how she came to Plymouth. She has often told me bits of her history when I have been staying with her at her lodgings, at Trafalgar Place, Stoke, Devonport.

Her father was a gentleman of the county of Kent, and a landed proprietor. (I believe the family residence is now occupied by the eldest son's son.) Mrs. Reed was the eldest of sixteen children. When grown to womanhood, she married a Captain Reed. They lived together for nearly two years ; then Major Reed was ordered with his regiment (the 48th) to Gibraltar. Their first baby was buried at Chester.

Mrs. Reed's father and mother were very unwilling she should go to Gibraltar with her husband, as they felt it beneath their daughter to be following the regiment, but wished her to stay at their home, which arrangement was agreed to amongst them. So their own home was given up. Major Reed wished to see his wife safely under her father's protection, so they were staying there till it was time for him to start. They were all sitting at dinner one evening, when Major

Reed looked his wife in the face, and said, "My dear, did you and I come together to be parted, as we shall be to-morrow?" She did not speak for a few moments, and then said to him, "No, my dear husband, and I will go with you, even if it be to the great sorrow and dismay of my parents." All was at once arranged for their starting the next day to Gibraltar, which they did. They landed safely; but it was only one week before Major Reed was taken ill with brain fever, caused by sunstroke, and in another week he was dead. Mrs. Reed was borne up wonderfully. She buried him, and in one month from their landing she was again placed in the same steamer that had brought them out, for her passage home without him. I have heard her say that when she got quiet in the steamer, and had time to consider all the matter, her poor mind and body were borne down by it. But she was always very, very thankful that she had gone with him to Gibraltar.

She remained at home for some months. By this time some of Mr. Philpot's family were living at Stoke, near Plymouth. They had always been friendly, as Mr. Philpot's father was the clergyman of Mrs. Reed's father's parish. Hearing of Mrs. Reed's trial, and knowing the state of her mind spiritually, from a letter they had received from her (for by this time she was converted), they invited her down to Stoke to spend a month with them. She came down by steamer from Southampton. On the way from the Barbican to their house the sun was just rising on a June morning, and these words came to her—" But unto you that fear My name shall the Sun of Righteousoess arise with healing in His wings." She prayed earnestly that the Sun of Righteousness might arise with healing to her soul. She stood for a few moments to consider the matter, and then, by faith, she was enabled, through the Spirit's teaching, to see Jesus as being all her salvation and all her desire. After this she went on to her friend's house at Higher Stoke with her soul set at liberty, rejoicing in Christ Jesus, and having no confidence in the flesh. There she spent the month for which she was invited.

The Philpots took her about to the different places of worship. She found a Mr. Easterbrook, of Devonport, an Independent minister. His preaching was wonderfully blest to her soul, and she felt she would wish to remain under his ministry for a time. So she took lodgings at Stoke, and remained there for about eight years, and continued under Mr. Easterbrook's ministry, but heard others occasionally. She soon found others who loved the Word of God among the poor of the Lord's people, and had a little circle of religious friends, who would often visit her and she them. All this was more joy to her present state of mind than all the gaiety and grandeur of her father's house. She had only a few acquaintances among those in her own station of life. Among these were Mrs. Tolcher, a lady at Newnham, the other side of Plymouth. She was a Christian, and used to ride into Plymouth to hear Mr. Triggs. Here Mrs. Reed became acquainted with her. These two soon found that they had one heart and one mind in the things of Jesus, and they were great friends till Mrs. Tolcher's death. Dr. and Mrs. Bullteel, of Plymouth, Mrs. Reed was also friendly with.

Mrs. Reed had been at Stoke about two years when she first saw me. After that, she became acquainted with my mother, and continued her friend for three years. Then my mother died, and she became my great friend (as I have mentioned before) up to the time of her leaving Stoke, and going to another part of England. Why she left Stoke in the first place was because her father wrote to her, and said that he and her mother were going to Hastings for a month, and if she would come and join them he would pay all her expenses. She did so, and when the month was up she desired to go to Camberwell for a month, to hear Mr. Irons. She went there and took lodgings, and attended his ministry for two months, after which she moved to Welwyn, in Hertfordshire. There she met Mr. Smart, and married him in January, 1848.

The two following letters of Mrs. Reed's have been preserved, one written to Mrs. Andrew, and one to Miss Andrew :—

AFFLICTION THE LOT OF GOD'S SAINTS.

(No date.)

"MY DEAR FRIEND,—I have long been waiting to hear from you. Last week my mind was disposed to make up a parcel for you, and as I seemed in such haste to do it, I thought you must be coming on Saturday. However, your letter decided that point. I was sorry to find by it that Jane has fresh afflictions, but as she acknowledges the hand whence they come, I trust she will be able to follow the exhortation of the Apostle, and 'count them all joy'; and that 'when patience has had its perfect work,' she may be found perfect and entire, lacking nothing. I have thought much of your communication to me when we last met, but it appears you are as much in the dark as I am relative to the issue. Of one thing you may be satisfied—it cannot be received by any of the parties, if you and your brother are next-of-kin, without your signature ; the lawyers will take care of that. Oh, my dear friend, none but the children of God know the perplexing path of a Christian ! The world can act for themselves, but the Christian must stand still and commit his way unto the Lord, and wait till He is pleased to move before him, and show him the way he should take. And yet it is better to wait all our days on the Lord, even if He seem not to regard us, than to take our own way. These struggles at a throne of grace are not without their sanctifying influence on the soul, if I may speak from experience; and I do think I know something about it. My weak state

of health causes me many heart-searchings. I cannot
but believe I have a living hope, which is cast as an
anchor within the veil, entering beyond the flesh of
the dear Redeemer even unto the living God, who is
the hope of Israel, and the Saviour thereof in all their
times of trouble. Ah! and it is in times of trouble
that we experience the blessedness of having something more than self in the world to rest upon. I was
struck with the following passage in Bunyan the other
day—'Did we heartily renounce the pleasures of this
world, we should be very little troubled for our afflictions; that which renders an afflicted state so insup-
portable to many is because they are too much
addicted to the pleasures of this life, and so cannot
endure that which makes a separation between them.'
Is it not so? And what more calculated than bodily
infirmities to wean us from earth and all its vanities?
The more I examine and ponder over these things,
the more I observe that sickness, more or less, is
generally the lot of God's saints; and as sickly, but
highly-favoured Toplady says, 'We are bad enough
with all our troubles; what should we be without
them?' Young Timothy had a weak stomach, and
'oft infirmities.' I think I can, in some measure, enter
into your feelings while waiting the issue of the little
property your brother is litigating, begging the Lord,
doubtless, that if you should have an increase to your
little means, He will give you wisdom to use it rightly;
and should your expectations be disappointed, you
may have grace patiently to submit to His will. I
need not say how glad I shall be to see you when you
can come. I was thinking last week we had spent
some pleasant, and, I trust, profitable hours together;
and should my life be spared beyond yours, I believe
I shall find your trials, which the Lord has brought
you through, a strength to my soul in trying scenes
and circumstances which may yet be before me.

"Friend Organ is well. He desired me to tell you
he was alive, and that was all he could say; notwith-

standing, I hope this winter has had fewer trials than many he has passed through. He looks cheerful and comfortable, and if it be the Lord's will, I hope his latter end may be better than the beginning.

"Is this mild weather favourable for your crops? You know I like to hear how your farm thrives, how many little pigs you have, and such things, as I feel interested in all that concerns you.

"Mr. Courtnay is very bad. What a change his death will make in the religious world of Plymouth!

"Have you heard from your son John lately? Remember me to Jane; tell her she improves in her writing.

"With affectionate love to yourself, I can only say I am, as ever,

"Faithfully your friend,

"ELIZABETH REED.

"To Mrs. Andrew."

SPIRITUAL FORTITUDE.

December 26th, 1844.

"MY DEAR JANE,—I have perused your letter with much pleasure, and can well enter into the workings of your mind. They are painful; nevertheless, they are profitable. To *say*, 'We can do nothing,' is very easy; but O! to *feel* is quite another thing. Yet the Lord will have experimental, not theoretical witnesses for His truths, and when you find (I know the very spot where I came to this conclusion from cutting experience) you cannot raise even one good thought to save your soul from hell, you must, if saved, declare salvation is all of grace. You say you can trust the Lord with your soul, but cannot trust Him for your daily supplies. Perhaps, if you were on the verge of

Jordan, and knew it must be crossed in a few hours, you might have some misgivings about eternal things. Temporals call for a continued exercise of faith; eternals are not always so pressing. And yet how sweetly has the sympathising Jesus considered our infirmities (Luke xii., 22nd to 32nd verse), but alas! alas! we are fools, and slow of heart to believe, and so, I fear, we shall be to the end.

I heard from John,* I think, on the same day that George did, but I waited for your letter until I informed you. He sent very clear directions for the payment of the money, and made no observation respecting the 6s. 8d. or any other disposal of it. I forwarded the whole to my brother by the next post. I have not heard from him. I suppose I shall not till after the Christmas holidays, when he will attend to it; and I hope a few mails will inform me the money has been safely received. John desired his love to his brothers and sister, and said he had written to George and Richard.

"I did not, my dear Jane, intend to reprove you, but merely to quicken you, lest you should murmur. I feel for your forlorn situation, and like you to tell me all your troubles. If I cannot remove them, I may instrumentally endeavour to direct your mind in a right channel. I thought you would find some sweet morsels in Luther; we live in days when we have need to beg the Lord to give us a little of his fortitude. I read Luther when I was situated as you are. I have reason to think I had never conversed with a Christian, nor heard anything like Gospel; and his determined spirit was very kindred with that boldness the Lord had wrought in me, to abide by His testimony in the face of all opposition. I used to think thus—I think I can feel a little of the spirit now—'Luther had the very spirit of Paul, and I have the spirit of Luther!' I walked about like a giant

* This was John Andrew, of Canada, and probably refers to the £20 left by Mrs. Andrew to each of her children.

refreshed with new wine, and really counted all things as loss for the excellency of the knowledge of Christ Jesus the Lord. Many times since have I sighed for those days. Yet, blessed be the God and Father of every mercy, I believe it was the Spirit of Christ which operated in Paul, Luther, and me, and I humbly hope in you also; and as I used then often to take sweet comfort from these words, so I say now, 'He that has begun a good work'—and I cannot but think He has—'will carry it on until the day of Jesus Christ.'

"You have not told me how much honey I have—whether you filled both jars, and whether I have sent money enough. How tiresome to return to such beggarly things! Yet, while we have flesh and blood, we must make some provision for them. Happy day when mortality shall be swallowed up of life! There is nothing really worth living for but Christ; and to fully enjoy Him we must die—or be changed, if the day of judgment find us alive, 'in a moment, in the twinkling of an eye.' What so instantaneous! It seems as if the Apostle could not find words to express the suddenness. I have felt a little sweetness in writing, my dear Jane, and I hope you may in reading my thoughts just as they flowed,-and then you will join with me in ascribing all praise to Him who alone could produce one Christian thought or desire. And may Father, Son, and Holy Ghost, one God in Covenant, be increasingly precious to our souls, is the prayer of

"Your sincere friend,

"ELIZABETH REED.

"To Miss Jane Andrew."

W. H. and L. COLLINGRIDGE, 148 and 149, Aldersgate Street, London, E.C.